VENICE *ITALY*
COOKING
WITH BETTY EVANS

For Vivian
Salute
Betty Evans

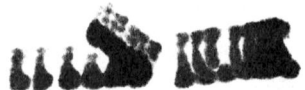

VENICE *ITALY* COOKING

With Betty Evans

Art by Gordon Evans

ACKNOWLEDGEMENTS

Thanks to Jean Salvadore and Luciano Parolari of the Villa d'Este for sharing their food and ideas along our route to Venice; to Herbert and Elsie Zoll for the memories of Italian classes we shared at the Universita per stranieri in Perugia. Grazie to the late Louis Monza for teaching me how to make polenta, the restaurant Al Theatro for always adding an extra table under the stars for us, Jack and Pat Belasco for joining our Venice walks and evenings, my great friend Joan Clark for giving me the Platina Venice cookbook, Harry Cipriani for his fabulous Venice food and high standards, and Agnes Steiner at La Calcina for being so nice to us. Again thanks to M.F.K. Fisher who is such a terrific lady and always inspires me, and Ric and Billie Masten for wanting another book. Grazie tanto to my husband Gordon who sketched and waited patiently while I read and studied Venice menus.

(paperback) 9 8 7 6 5 4 3 2

Copyright © 1986 by Betty Evans

All rights reserved. No part of this work may be reproduced or transmitted in any form by any means, electronic or mechanical. Including photocopying and/or recording, or by any information storage or retrieval system, without permission in writing from the publisher.

Library of Congress Catalogue Card No. 86-061768

ISBN 0-931104-18-1

For Gordon, Bob, Suzanne and Jeanne who share the memories of our first gondola ride.

FOREWORD

Every one of us is a citizen of Venice, whether it be the fabulous Venice of painting, music and literature, or the scintillating reality we can see from a gondola or touch as we cross one of her low-arched bridges. Venice is simply the most beautiful, human-scaled and irresistible city the world has ever created.

It is a spiritual republic, too, not a kingdom or an aristocratic fief. The celebrities and ex-royalties who flock there have not an ounce more domain over it than any of the rest of us who love her dearly. And the superb cuisine of Venice, which Betty Evans describes so effectively in this little book, is not a grand, courtly cuisine, but the simple, earthy cooking of ordinary people—people, mind you, with eight or nine hundred years of experience in cooking the superlative seafood and rice and vegetables and fruit of the Venetian territory.

Most of us have our own vivid memories of time spent in Venice. I recall a frosty December in Venice, and watching a priest and censer-swinging acolytes accompany a coffin across *Piazza San Marco* to a waiting hearse-gondola; an evening in the tiny bar of a hotel when Massino, the precocious six-year-old son of an opera singer warbling Mozart at that very moment in Venice's exquisite opera house, *La Fenice,* insisted on joining us and bringing a handful of fresh ice cubes every few minutes for our drinks; a simple *trattoria* along the *Rialto* with the radio tuned in to excellent chamber music; "Our patrons insist on this kind of music;" a private supper club in the beam-crossed attic-loft of an old *palazzo*, with candlelight, fine crystal and silver but the same succulent *risottos* and *fegato Veneziano* and *polenta* and *calamari* served in the most modest restaurants. Great, memorable meals, and exactly the same cooking for everyone, of low or high degree. *Brava, Venezia!*

—*Kirk McDonald*

PREFACE

I have a map of Venice on the wall in my room because I have a fascination with maps. A map of Venice is very unique. The streets are all water. Venice is actually 118 little islands with about 400 bridges to connect them. The "S" shape of the Grand Canal is the ancient deep channel that makes it possible to enter Venice from the open sea. The long, slim sand island Lido protects Venice from the assault of the Adriatic. Without this protection there could not be a Venice.

Venice began because there have always been people searching for a safe place to live. Barbarians were ravishing the Adriatic coast in the fifth century. Fugitives moved out into the lagoon. They first settled on the island of Torcello. From there they slowly moved out further to the islands that today make up the city of Venice. They sunk oak piles into the clay islands to support homes. When you are in Venice you will see many arches and large open areas in buildings. This is to ease the weight on this forest of pilings that holds up the palaces and lacy structures. Tides swish in and out of the canals twice a day. It is a fragile environment.

My interest in Venice began at an early age, I think about four. My grandpa would show me pictures in the National Geographic. I can remember seeing Venice and wanting to ride in a gondola and walk across the bridges.

In 1956 my husband and I decided to sell our Hermosa Beach home and all the odds and ends that go in a house. We planned to take the proceeds and spend it on living in Italy until the money ran out. He wanted to paint and I wanted to cook and visit Etruscan places. We had our three children with us. They helped to show us many things in Italy with their youth and innocence we would not have experienced without them.

The first April we were in Italy we made our Venice visit. I got to ride in a gondola and walk over the bridges.

That first gondola ride was very memorable. The gondolier most gallantly helped all five of us into his gondola. We were off among the canals. The ride is quiet and smooth. We saw all the sights along the Grand Canal and went under the Bridge of Sighs. As we were approaching the end of our hour-long excursion the gondolier made a proposal to us. For a most modest price he offered to take us in his gondola over to the island of Murano to see the glass factories. Of course we said yes and soon were in the open lagoon. Venice was fading behind us and there was just water all around. It was exciting and very beautiful. I thought those first Venetians were brave to settle like the poet Cassiodorus said, "Here you live like sea birds scattered over a watery expanse." It is when you are in a gondola in the lagoon that you sense the complete helpless frailty of this city.

The glass factory was noisy and busy. The factories were made to move to this island from Venice for fear of fires. On the gondola ride back, it was magic to see Venice emerge from the sea and soon we were back walking over bridges and eating for dinner a big "Fritto Misto and grilled polento." There was a salad of radicchio, a chilled dry local white wine and gelati for everyone. It was then that I had the idea to start collecting ideas and recipes from Venice.

The food of Venice is bewitching, the colors are sensuous, and the ingredients are freshly plucked from the sea or from the gardens on the mainland. They are put together in a marvelous, easy way. There is a romance of spices weaved in and out of the flavors. Venice did supply the world with spices. Ships for the Crusades left from Venice to the Holy Land. Marco Polo left for his long trip to China. All these influences are mingled in the Venetian menu. The famous liver dish "Fegato alla Veneziana" is cut Oriental style and stir fried. Plump raisins, cinnamon, pine nuts, ginger, saffron and capers are tucked into the cuisine of Venice.

The dining experience in Venice is refreshing. In warm weather tables are flung out and tablecloths draped across them. If they are filled you will not wait because another table will be found and added just for you. Perhaps this casual, breezy mood is because there is water all around you. In the streets and piazza are water sounds. There are boats, birds, ripples, splashes and the lapping of oars. All this is mingled with that beautiful Italian language. In Venice both the ears and eyes are in for a treat.

Inside of the restaurants the debonair waiters will show you to a table with a gracious gesture. As you pass to your table you will see the antipasti. There are dishes of fresh seafood, marinated vegetables, and roasted peppers waiting for you. Your wine is poured and the menu is in your hand. The curtain is about to go up for Venice is like a theatre. Dining is one of the acts. I want to return again for an encore.

Betty Evans
Hermosa Beach, California
1986

TABLE OF CONTENTS

APPETIZERS

Prosciutto with bread sticks, 3
Chicken livers on toast, 4
Sardine fingers, 5
Hard-boiled eggs stuffed with spinach, 6
Prosciutto with melon, 7
Little shrimp toast, 8
Fried cheese, 9
Beef raw filet with mustard sauce, 10

SOUPS

Venetian bean soup, 13
Pavese style soup, 14
Bean and pasta soup, 15
Celery, rice and sausage soup, 16
Barley and bean soup, 17
Chicken broth with cheese cubes, 18

SALADS

Romaine salad with red onions, 21
Russian salad, 22
Tomato and basil Summer salad, 23
Veneto string bean salad, 24
Mixed salad, 25
Lettuce with farmer's dressing, 26

MEAT AND POULTRY

Little beef steaks with red onions, 29
Beef roast cooked in red wine, 30
Flat Italian meatballs with lemon, 31
Veal cooked in lemon and wine sauce, 32
Pork cooked in milk, 33
Pork chops with wine and lemon, 34
Escaped birds, 35
Chicken breasts with prosciutto and cheese, 36

Grilled Venetian chicken, 37
Duck with lemon pepper sauce, 38
Liver Venetian style, 39
Tongue with sweet and sour raisin sauce, 40

FISH AND SEAFOOD

Sea bass cooked in white wine, 43
Shrimp with lemon and garlic, 44
Shrimps in a Parmesan sauce, 45
Venetian crab salad, 46
Mixed fry of the sea, 47
Grilled fish, 48
Venetian savory sole, 49

PASTA, POLENTA AND RICE

A note about risotto, 53
Classic risotto, 54
Rice and peas Venice style, 55
Polenta recipes, 56
Basic polenta, 57
Polenta with mushroom sauce, 58
Spaghettini with peas, eggs and prosciutto, 59
Baked lasagna, 60

VEGETABLES

Grandmother's style zucchini, 63
Spinach with golden raisins, 64
Fried zucchini, 65
Sauced asparagus, 66
Sweet and sour onions, 67
Mashed potatoes with Parmesan cheese, 68
Mushrooms with garlic, 69

PIZZA AND SANDWICHES

Pizza in Venice, 73
Venetian pizza toppings, 74
Sandwiches, 75
Venetian sandwich fillings, 76

DESSERTS

Chocolate and walnut cake, 79
Pears filled with cheese, 80
Venice style Sicilian cake, 81
Pears poached in red wine, 82
Macedonia of mixed fruit, 83
Yellow diamond cornmeal cookies, 84
Italian lemon pie, 85
Baked stuffed peaches, 86

VISITING VENICE, 89–91

**SUGGESTED HOTELS
AND RESTAURANTS IN VENICE,** 92–93

INDEX, 95

1. APPETIZERS -
Antipasti

PROSCIUTTO WITH BREAD STICKS
Prosciutto e Grissini

There is a very special happy mood on those bright, sunlit days in Venice. Everyone seems to be eating outside. Enjoying lunch in one of the many Venice restaurants under sunny skies is a fantastic experience. These are the times when people watching is especially fun. On one of these days I found myself intrigued while observing a group of healthy, husky, athletic-looking young men. Course upon course was served them, each one with additional bottles of wine. When the first course, was served the waiter brought a large platter of sliced prosciutto with a basket of bread sticks. The men would take a slice of prosciutto and wrap it around the bread stick. They would hold this in their hands and nibble the stick enjoying it along with their wine. This is certainly one of the easiest and fun ways to start a meal.

Prosciutto sliced very thin
breadsticks

The amount will depend on how many people you are serving. Two or three sticks is usually the right amount for one serving. You may buy the prosciutto in the amount you need. Keep it tightly wrapped so it will not dry out. To prepare, simply place the prosciutto on a platter with a fork and the bread sticks in a basket. Of course, if your guests are lazy, you may prepare the dish by simply wrapping one slice of the ham around one breadstick.

CHICKEN LIVERS ON TOAST
Crostini di Fegatini di Pollo

Crostini are pieces of white bread toasted or fried on one side and then spread with various mixtures. This chicken liver mixture is on many Venice menus reflecting the traditional Venetian love of liver.

½ lb fresh chicken livers
2 T. butter
1 T. olive oil
1 green onion, minced
1 tsp. dried or fresh sage, minced fine
1 T. red or white wine
salt and pepper to taste
parsley for garnish
6 white bread slices

Melt the butter and oil in a frying pan. Cut the livers in quarters for faster cooking. This is easily done with scissors. Cook the livers with the onion and sage until slightly pink inside. Do not overcook as they will be tough. Season to taste with salt and pepper. Add wine to the pan at the last minute and stir around. Remove to a bowl and mash with a fork. Spread on crostini. Crostini are made by buttering one slice of bread and toasting - or fry in a little butter and olive oil on one side and drain on paper towels. You may cut these in any desired shape. Spread with the chicken liver mixture. Garnish with parsley. This will serve 3-4.

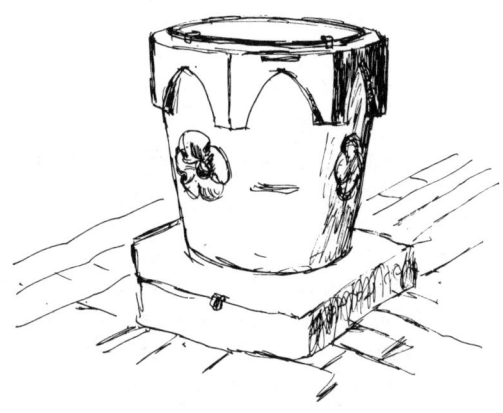

SARDINE FINGERS
Detti Sardo

The Italian cuisine has many whimsical names like "sardine fingers." These make a fun, tasty appetizer. Sardines are full of calcium and very healthy.

> 1 can of tiny sardines (3¾ oz)
> 6 slices of firm white bread
> Parmesan cheese
> black pepper
> parsley for garnish
> butter

Remove the crusts from the bread. Cut into narrow strips (about 3x2). These are the fingers. Butter and toast on one side. You may do this under a broiler. Some Italians simply fry the bread lightly in a mixture of olive oil and butter (in a frying pan). The reason for toasting on one side is to give strength and taste to the bread.

Sprinkle the parmesan cheese on a plate and mix with some freshly ground black pepper. Roll the sardines in the cheese mixture. Place one sardine on each "finger." Place under a medium broiler flame for just a minute to lightly brown the sardines. Place on a plate. Garnish with parsley and serve while warm. You may do the preparation ahead and pop the fingers under the broiler when your guests arrive. This will serve 4.

HARD-BOILED EGGS STUFFED WITH SPINACH
Uova sode Agli Spinaci

    I love the mixed green and yellow colors sitting in the white halves of the eggs. This recipe looks so fresh and pretty and the taste is wonderful. Spinach-stuffed eggs can be part of an Antipasto platter or served alone for lunches and picnics.

12 eggs, hard boiled
1-10 oz pkg of chopped frozen spinach - or 1 bunch of fresh (cooked and chopped)
salt and pepper to taste
¼ cup mayonnaise
2 T. olive oil
2 T. grated Parmesan cheese
salt and pepper to taste

    Cook the spinach. Drain and squeeze dry. This is important as excess spinach juice is not desirable in this dish.
    Carefully shell the eggs. Separate the yolks from the whites. Mash the yolks with the spinach, mayonnaise, oil, cheese and salt and pepper. Fill each egg white with the yolk mixture. Try and do this carefully so that the white of the egg does not have the filling dribbling over it. The beauty of the dish is the pristine look of the white against the green-yellow color. Chill covered with foil or plastic wrap until serving time.

PROSCIUTTO AND MELON
Prosciutto e melon

A slice of colorful melon draped with a thin slice of prosciutto is one of the loveliest and most refreshing of Italian appetizers. You may use any melon. Cantalope seems to be the favorite. This may be because an Italian pope planted some melon seeds which were brought to him from Armenia in the Papal gardens at Cantalupo near Rome. This melon that flourished in this area is called Cantalupo after the town name.

1 ripe melon chilled
6-8 paper thin slices of Prosciutto (about ¼ lb)
black pepper freshly ground (optional)

Cut the melon into 6 to 8 crescent-shaped pieces. You may peel the melon if desired. Carefully remove the seeds. Place the slices on a dish and lay the prosciutto over each slice. Serve with the pepper, if you like pepper. This will serve 4.

LITTLE SHRIMP TOAST
Crostini Scampi

This is one of my favorite of Venetian little first courses. One reason I like it is that if you have some unexpected guests this is very easy to assemble and your guests will be delighted. Try and keep a package of those little cleaned bay shrimp in your freezer along with some bread so you're ready for company.

½ lb small shrimp, cooked and cleaned
¼ cup grated Parmesan cheese
2 T. fresh lemon juice
½ tsp. dried or fresh thyme leaves
1 T. minced parsley
½ cup mayonnaise
salt and pepper to taste
1 tsp. Capers, minced
6 bread slices toasted lightly and buttered

Chop the shrimp medium fine—you want a tiny texture and not a mush. Add the cheese, lemon, thyme, capers, and salt and pepper. Blend in the mayonnaise and mix together. This may be done ahead and kept refrigerated. Toast the bread. Sometimes the crusts are removed; this is up to you.

Spread the shrimp mixture evenly on the toast. Place on a baking sheet and bake at 350 degrees until the crostini are hot and bubbly.

Cut in half and serve at once. This goes well with a chilled white Soave wine. Garnish with a small bunch of grapes if desired. This will serve 3.

FRIED CHEESE
Formaggio Fritto

This appetizer is a good choice for cool evenings. It is a little messy to eat, so serve on little plates with a napkin. Fried cheese is very satisfying and typically Venetian with the corn meal (polenta) coating.

½ lb of a soft cheese (Muenster, Mozzarella or Jack)
1 egg beaten
1 cup cornmeal
salt and pepper to taste

Olive oil for frying, about ¼ cup (can be half peanut or corn oil)

Cut the cheese into strips about ½ inch thick and about 2½ inches long. Beat the egg and spread the cornmeal on a paper towel or wax paper.

Heat the oil in a frying pan. Dip the cheese into the egg and then the cornmeal. Carefully fry one side until golden brown and then turn on the other side. Fry just until the cheese is melted (about a minute on each side). Season with salt and pepper and serve.

You may coat the cheese ahead so when your guests arrive all you have to do is give a quick fry and serve. Drain on paper towels and serve immediately. This will make 2 generous servings.

BEEF RAW FILET WITH MUSTARD SAUCE
Filetto di bue alla Carpaccio

Carpaccio is a favorite on the menus of Venice. It is thin raw beef slices with a zappy mustard sauce. This combination of flavors is quite a taste sensation. Sometimes it is served with the sauce in a mound in the center of the dish. At the famous "Locando Cipriani" on the lagoon island of Torcello, the sauce was arranged on the beef in a lattice form of design.

1 lb beef filet (top sirloin works well)
1 cup prepared or homemade mayonnaise
3 T. Dijon style mustard
2 tsp. fresh lemon juice
4 sprigs of parsley

Freeze the meat for 30 minutes. This is just to make it firm enough to slice very thin. Do not do this until the day you are making the dish. The meat should be frozen, sliced and served for the freshness of the dish.

Place the meat on a board. With a very sharp knife slice very thin and arrange the slices overlapping on a plate.

The sauce is made by combining the mayonnaise, lemon and mustard. Stir and blend well. ¼ of a pound of the filet is the amount for each serving. This may be served on individual plates or from a platter. Arrange the sauce in a pretty round mound, or like Harry does in a lattice fashion. This will serve 4. A sprig of parsley can be added as a garnish.

2. SOUPS -
Minestre

VENETIAN BEAN SOUP
Zuppa alla Veneto

A hearty bowl of steaming bean soup is perfect for those days in Venice when the mist and fog roll in. The city looks mysterious and the trattoria windows are steamy.

> *1-16 oz package dry red beans*
> *2 quarts of water*
> *2 onions, chopped*
> *2 fresh cloves of garlic, minced*
> *1 bay leaf*
> *½ cup diced Prosciutto*
> *olive oil*
> *salt and pepper to taste*

Soak the beans overnight in water. All the beans should be covered. Drain the beans and place in a pot with the onion, garlic, salt and pepper and prosciutto. Simmer covered until the beans are tender. Remove 2 cups of the beans and mash. You will have to let the beans cool slightly for easier handling. Return the beans to the soup pot and stir to blend.

In each soup bowl pour a little dash of olive oil and sprinkle with black pepper. Pour in the soup and enjoy. This will serve 6.

PAVESE STYLE SOUP
Zuppa Pavese

When you are visiting Italy you will often hear a phrase "sono stanco." This simply means I am tired. This popular soup in the Northern regions of the country is the solution to a tired feeling. A bowl of Pavese will pep you up and the stanco feeling will be gone.

According to history this soup was created in 1525 when the defeated King Francis of France was wandering around the Pavese countryside hungry. He arrived at a farmhouse where the farmer's wife was making a simple soup. She offered him a bowl and when he said he was a king she added an egg to make the soup fit for a king.

6 cups of rich beef or chicken stock or broth
4 eggs
4 slices of white bread
grated Parmesan cheese

Heat the stock or broth to boiling. Turn down the flame to medium. Break the eggs one by one in a cup and slide into the soup. When each egg is poached carefully remove it and set aside. Place pieces of bread in the bowl. Pour in the soup and add the eggs. Sprinkle with Parmesan cheese. This will make 4 large bowls.

BEAN AND PASTA SOUP
Zuppa di pasta e fagioli

There are many versions of bean and pasta soup. In Venice it is usually made with white beans and thin, curly lasagna noodles. You may use, of course, any style of pasta you want. This soup is very nourishing, easy and inexpensive to make. You can always freeze part of the soup to have on hand for a chilly night.

1 lb Navy or Northern white beans
1 cup dry pasta (can be any shape)
1 ham hock or 1 country style pork spare rib
1 onion, chopped
1 celery stalk, chopped
1 carrot, chopped
1 clove garlic, minced
salt and pepper to taste
1-8 oz can tomato sauce
minced parsley and Parmesan cheese for garnish

Soak the beans overnight. This makes them cook easily and prevents splitting. Place the beans in a soup pot and cover with 2 quarts of water. Add the onion, celery, carrot, garlic, and ham or pork. Season with salt and pepper and stir in the tomato sauce. Cook covered over a low flame until the beans are tender. This will take an hour. You don't want them mushy. Remove the ham or pork. Cut into little pieces and return to the soup. Bring the soup to a simmer. Add the pasta and cook until the pasta is tender—about ten minutes. If you use curly lasagna noodles, break them in small pieces. The thin kind are best. If the soup is too thick for your taste, add some white wine to thin it. Garnish with the cheese and parsley. This will serve 8.

CELERY, RICE AND SAUSAGE SOUP
Minestra de sedano e riso con salsicce

Celery is a very popular vegetable in Venice because it grows in the Po Valley and surrounding countryside. This celery is very flavorful and used in many Venetian dishes. I like this thick, hearty soup on foggy days.

2 T. butter
1 onion, chopped
2 Italian sausages (about ½ lb), can be hot or sweet
4 cups chicken broth
½ cup white wine
1½ cups diced celery
salt and pepper to taste
½ cup short grain rice
¼ cup Parmesan cheese and 2 T. minced parsley for garnish

In a soup pot melt the butter and add the onion. Remove the casing from the sausage and crumble. Add the sausage to the onion and stir fry a few minutes until the onion becomes limp. Add the broth and the wine with salt and pepper to taste. Now add the diced celery. Cover and cook for 30 minutes. Add the rice and cook for an additional 20 minutes. The rice should not be overcooked. Serve the soup garnished with Parmesan cheese and a little minced parsley. This will serve 4-5.

BARLEY AND BEAN SOUP
Zuppa de fagioli e orzo

There is something so intriguing about the idea of beans and barley in the same soup. This combination is on several Venice menus. It is not only very flavorful, but has a texture that is unique and delicious.

> 1 cup small pink or red beans
> 1 cup barley
> 1 onion, chopped
> 3 slices of bacon, diced
> 2½ quarts of water (approximately)
> ½ cup white wine
> salt and pepper to taste
> pinch of cinnamon (optional)
> Parmesan cheese and minced parsley for garnish

Soak the beans in water to cover overnight or for a few hours. In a soup pot place the diced bacon and lightly brown with the chopped onions. Add the wine and stir. Next add the water, beans, salt and pepper. Cook covered for 30 minutes. Add the barley and cook an additional 30 minutes or until the barley and beans are tender. You do not want them overcooked. Add the cinnamon if desired; this adds a little dash is an idea leftover from the days of the spice trade. Garnish each bowl with Parmesan cheese and some minced parsley. This will serve 6.

CHICKEN BROTH WITH CHEESE CUBES
Brodo di pollo con cubetti

This is a delicate lovely soup. You might serve it for a summer lunch or as a first course for an elegant dinner. The cheese cubes are made like a little pudding, cooled and then cut in small cubes. The hot broth is then poured over the cubes.

6 cups hot chicken broth
1½ cups ricotta
1 green onion, minced
1 T. minced fresh parsley
2 eggs, beaten
salt and pepper to taste
pinch of nutmeg

Combine the ricotta, green onion, parsley and eggs with seasonings. Mix well and place in a square baking pan. Place this pan in another larger pan containing water. Making a sort of an oven double boiler. Bake at 300 degrees for 20-25 minutes until the pudding is firm. Let cool. You may refrigerate it overnight if desired. When ready to serve, heat the broth to boiling. Place the cubes evenly between 4 soup bowls. Heat the broth to boiling and pour over the cubes. This will serve 4.

3. SALADS -
Insalata

ROMAINE SALAD WITH RED ONION
Insalata di lattuga rosso cipolle

Colorful and tasty salads are part of the Venice scene. This simple salad with its red onion rings is always a lovely addition to any meal. When I first lived in Italy, I was surprised to see that my Italian landlady, Signora Pia, threw away all the outer leaves of romaine lettuce. She only used the inside tender leaves and this is what makes this salad so pretty and tasty.

> *1 bunch of romaine lettuce*
> *1 medium size red onion*
> *½ cup lightly toasted walnuts*
> *5 T. olive oil and 2 T. wine vinegar with*
> *salt and pepper to taste*

I know you may feel guilty, but discard all those outer leaves of a romaine lettuce head. Maybe a neighbor has a rabbit you can feed them to. Wash and tear the leaves in pieces. Place in a towel and refrigerate until it is time to make the salad. Cut the onion in slices. Coarsely chop the walnuts. Place the onions and walnuts in a salad bowl. Season with salt and pepper. Add the olive oil and wine vinegar and toss. Serve at once. This will serve 4.

RUSSIAN SALAD
Insalata al Russa

I had always been curious what Russian salad was doing on menus in Italian restaurants. Russian salad is a potato salad with vegetables added. The salad is marinated in an oil and vinegar dressing, and just before serving mayonnaise is blended into the salad. Sometimes some slivered tounge or roast beef is added. A little scoop of this salad is often added to an antipasto plate. There are many uses for this popular salad. No, it isn't really Russian. The salad was the creation of Baron Reuss's cook. The baron was a foreign diplomat living in Italy. Somehow the name got changed from Reuss to Russa.

4 cups cooked diced potatoes (use white, rose or red)
1 cup cooked peas
1 cup cooked diced carrots
2 hard-boiled eggs, sliced
1 cup finely slivered tongue, beef or ham (optional)
salt and pepper to taste
$2/3$ cup of olive oil
$1/3$ cup wine vinegar
salt and pepper to taste
1 cup mayonnaise (approximately)
optional: capers, gherkins, cooked string beans
   or cauliflower

Place the potatoes, carrots, peas and eggs with meat, in a bowl. Blend the oil and vinegar together with salt and pepper. Mix well with the salad. Cover and refrigerate until time to serve. Just before serving blend in the mayonnaise. This will serve 6 as a salad course.

TOMATO AND BASIL SUMMER SALAD
Pomodori e basilico insalata di Estate

This is a summer salad. Don't dare to make it with wimpy winter tomatoes. You need red, juicy summer tomatoes and fresh green basil. This is the simplest and most satisfying of Italian salads. Provide some good sturdy bread for wiping up the tantalizing juices.

> *5 ripe tomatoes*
> *salt and pepper to taste*
> *¼ cup olive oil*
> *2 T. red wine vinegar*
> *10 fresh basil leaves (approximately)*
> *bread for dunking*

Slice the tomatoes about ¼ inch thick. Place on a pretty plate. Mix the olive oil, vinegar, salt and pepper. Snip the basil leaves in little pieces. Combine with the dressing and dribble over the tomatoes. With your hands or a fork gently squish the dressing around the tomatoes. Let stand 10-15 minutes so that the juices mellow. Do not make this salad ahead. It is to be made and enjoyed "pronto" at room temperature. This will serve 2. Sometimes slices of fresh mozzarella are added to the salad.

VENETO STRING BEAN SALAD
Insalata di fagiolini alla Veneto

Part of any Venice restaurant's summer listing for salads always includes this simple string bean salad. Of course string beans are available most of the year, but fresh beans from a summer garden are the best for this salad.

1 lb string beans
3 T. olive oil
1 T. wine vinegar
salt and pepper to taste
1 clove fresh garlic, peeled and minced
¼ cup finely chopped, lightly toasted walnuts
1 green onion, minced

Cut the ends from the beans and wash them. Cook 5-8 minutes in boiling, salted water to cover. You want the beans slightly crunchy. Mix all the ingredients except the walnuts in a bowl. Drain the beans and while still warm mix with the dressing ingredients. The beans soak up the flavor of the dressing using this method. To serve sprinkle the walnuts on top of the salad. This may be served at room temperature or chilled. This will serve 4.

MIXED SALAD
Insalata misto

This is the salad on most menus in Venice. It is simply a mixture of the fresh greens of the day. Sometimes grated carrot is added. The main attraction in Venice is Radicchio, which is a form of chickory. It grows near Venice and is the gem of Venice mixed salads. Radicchio is a small head of reddish-purple cabbage-like lettuce. The flavor is fresh and the texture is cool and slightly crunchy. When you visit the produce market you will see rows and rows of this Venice favorite. It is a beautiful sight you will not forget. Radicchio is beginning to become available is some American markets. The leaves make a sensational little cup to hold tidbits of many foods.

For a mixed salad simply clean and tear greens that are in season and that you like. Place them washed and drained on individual plates or bowls. Olive oil and wine vinegar is set on the table. Each person pours on what they want. Salt and pepper is also added to suit each individual taste.

LETTUCE WITH FARMER'S DRESSING
Insalata del fattore

Most salads in Venice are offered with olive oil and vinegar dressings. Gorgonzola cheese, however, is used in Venice for this "Farmer's dressing" and is very tasty.

1 head of any green lettuce
½ cup cream or half and half
¼ cup Gorgonzola or bleu cheese
½ cup olive oil
2 T. red wine vinegar
salt and pepper to taste

Wash and tear the leaves of the lettuce. I put them in a clean dish towel in the refrigerator to crisp.

In a bowl crumble the cheese. Slowly add the cream or half and half to make a creamy mixture. Blend in the oil and wine vinegar with salt and pepper. You may do this ahead, but give the dressing a good stir before adding to the salad. Arrange the lettuce in a bowl and pour the dressing over it. Toss and serve. This will serve 4.

4. MEAT & POULTRY -
Carne e Pollame

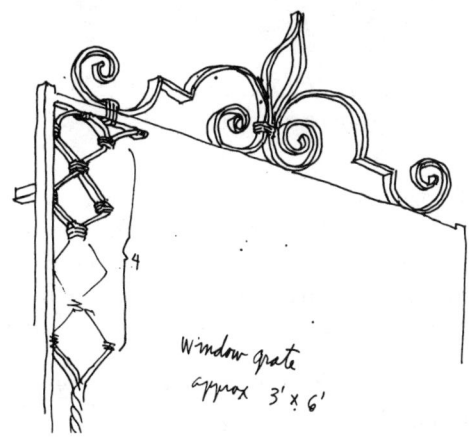

LITTLE BEEF STEAKS WITH RED ONIONS
Fettine di manzo cipollate

The Venetians are not big meat eaters because of all the abundant fresh fish in their city. Beef is expensive so they have invented a special recipe with small steaks. I find the flavor of the red onions with the steak a terrific combination.

> 1 lb red onions, peeled and sliced thin
> 3 T. olive oil
> 2 beef steaks (approximately ½ lb), sliced ½ inch thick
>   (top sirloin or New York recommended)
> 2 T. red wine
> parsley for garnish

In a heavy frying pan—I like iron pans—heat the olive oil, and over a low flame add the onions. Cook stirring for about 10 minutes. They should be tender and soft. With a slotted spoon remove the onions from the pan. There should be a little olive oil left in the pan; if not, add a little additional oil. Raise the flame to medium high. Brown the steaks on both sides. Season with salt and pepper. These steaks will cook quickly as they are thin. Remove from pan to a warm plate. Take the onions back to the pan with the wine. Swirl around for a minute. Pour the sauce over the steaks and serve garnished with parsley. This will serve 2.

A variation on this recipe is, after the steaks are cooked, to add a slice of mozzarella topped by a slice of tomato and pop under the broiler a minute to just barely melt the cheese.

BEEF ROAST COOKED IN RED WINE
Manzo al vino rosso

A tasty beef roast slowly cooked in red wine fills Venetian kitchens with rich aromas. This is not a dish for hot summer days. This is for the winter when Adriatic winds and rain are blowing and pelting outside. San Marco's square is empty. If you're lucky you can be in a warm restaurant enjoying this hearty dish.

> *4 lb beef roast (rump, bottom round or brisket)*
> *1 onion, chopped*
> *2 cloves garlic, minced*
> *3 slices bacon*
> *1 stalk celery, chopped*
> *1 carrot, chopped*
> *1-16 oz can of solid pack tomatoes*
> *1 bay leaf*
> *salt and pepper to taste*
> *3 T. olive oil*
> *4 cups red wine*

In a heavy pot that will fit the roast heat the oil. Cut the bacon in pieces and put in the pot with the onion, garlic, carrot and celery. Stir and fry until vegetables are limp. Remove the bacon and vegetables from the pan and add the roast. Brown the roast on all sides. Return the vegetables and bacon. Add the wine, tomatoes, salt and pepper, and bay leaf. You may now cook this in an oven at 325 degrees or on top of the stove over a low flame. It will take 2½ to 3 hours for the meat to be tender. I like the oven method. Check the pot once or twice during the cooking time to make sure there is plenty of liquid. I also like to break up any large tomato pieces. If you need more liquid add some more wine. Barola red wine is used for this dish in Venice, but any good dry red wine will do.

To serve remove roast to a platter. Reduce the liquid in the pan a little. The wine sauce may be strained if desired, but I like the texture of the vegetable bits. Serve the sauce in a bowl to spoon over the roast. This will serve 6 with some leftovers. Any leftover sauce can be used for soup.

FLAT ITALIAN MEATBALLS WITH LEMON
Polpette alla limone

Picnics are always a pleasure. There is nothing like the carefree feeling of tossing some tasty treats, a bottle of wine in a basket and heading for the outdoors. These flavorful meatballs are one of the perfect Italian picnic dishes. The lemon and parsley gives them a special Venetian flavor.

>   *1 lb lean ground beef*
>   *1 egg*
>   *1 slice of white bread*
>   *2 tsp. minced fresh parsley*
>   *salt and pepper to taste*
>   *grated rind of 1 lemon*
>   *pinch of nutmeg*
>   *1 clove garlic, minced*
>   *olive oil for frying*

In a bowl lightly beat the egg. Add the slice of bread and let it sit a few minutes to absorb the egg. Add the remaining ingredients and blend together. With your hands form the meat into flat cakes around ½ inch high and about 2½ inches in diameter. Heat the olive oil in a frying pan and brown the meat until golden brown on one side. Turn and brown on the other side. If you wish, these can be eaten hot. For picnics, chill and serve garnished with lemon wedges and parsley. This will make 6 cakes.

VEAL IN LEMON AND WINE SAUCE
Piccata di vitello

This combination of thin veal slices with a lemon sauce is one of the most delicate and refreshing dishes you can serve. Your guests will always be impressed. With the garnish of lemon and parsley it is most attractive and appealing.

1 lb veal cutlet
flour for dredging
3 T. butter
2 T. olive oil
salt and pepper to taste
juice of one medium-sized lemon
½ cup white wine
parsley and lemon slices or wedges for garnish

Pound the veal to about ¼ to ⅓ inch thick. Your butcher can do this for you, or you can do it with a meat pounder. Sprinkle flour on a piece of wax paper seasoned with salt and pepper.

In a frying pan heat the oil and butter. Brown the veal on both sides until golden brown. Do not overcook as veal is tender and does not need long cooking. Remove the veal from the pan and place in a warm spot. Add the lemon juice and wine to the pan and stir around to absorb the veal juices. Reduce slightly.

To serve place the veal on your serving plate and pour the sauce on top of the veal. Garnish with lemon wedges or slices and some minced parsley. This will serve 2.

PORK COOKED IN MILK
Arrosto de maiale al latte

I admit that this seemed a curious way to cook pork. You will be surprised; the pork is light and tender with a special flavor. Usually it is served hot; however, I have found that sliced cold it is lovely for picnic suppers.

1-3 to 4 lb loin of pork
2 cloves garlic, minced
1 onion, sliced
3 T. butter
salt and pepper to taste
4 to 5 cups milk
½ lb mushrooms, sliced and lightly browned in butter

Have your butcher bone and tie the roast for you. The bones can be saved for soups. In a heavy pot that will hold the roast, melt the butter. Lightly brown the onions and garlic, just until limp. Add the roast. Sprinkle with salt and pepper. Pour in the milk and cover. Simmer over a low flame, stirring now and then so nothing is sticking. If the milk gets too low, add a little more. The roast should be tender in about one to one-and-a-half hours. To serve, remove the roast, slice and pour the milk sauce over it. Garnish with parsley. Sometimes mushrooms are added to the milk sauce and served over the pork. This will serve 4 with some leftovers. I will caution you; the sauce may look grainy, but it is delicious. You might serve Parmesan mashed potatoes with this dish. The method of cooking pork in milk dates from a 15th-century Venetian cookbook.

PORK CHOPS WITH WINE AND LEMON
Braciole di maiale al vino e limone

This recipe is a refreshing way to prepare pork chops. They will be tangy and tender. The use of lemon is very popular in Venice and adds a terrific zap to foods.

> *4 center cut pork chops*
> *flour*
> *2 T. olive oil*
> *1 T. butter*
> *1 clove garlic, minced*
> *salt and pepper to taste*
> *2 T. fresh rosemary leaves (approximately)*
> *1 cup white wine*
> *juice of ½ lemon*

In a frying pan melt the butter and heat the oil. Rub flour into the pork chops. Brown lightly on both sides. Add the garlic and give a stir around. Pour in the juice and white wine. Season with salt and pepper. Add the rosemary leaves. Cover and cook for 20 minutes. Remove the cover. Stir and cook a minute or so to blend. Serve the chops with the sauce. This will serve 2.

ESCAPED BIRDS
Oseleti scapai

This recipe was invented by some clever Venetian lady. Her husband often returned from bird hunting empty handed and would tell her that the birds had escaped, so he didn't have any for their dinner. The men of Venice do like to hunt in the marshes of the lagoon islands. However, I suspect that it is more for a day out of the house with some friends than actual productive hunting. I don't like to eat little birds as I feel sorry for them, so this recipe is a good idea and quite tasty.

> *1 lb of chicken breast or veal cutlet*
> *½ lb chicken livers*
> *½ lb mushrooms*
> *6 slices of bacon*
> *olive oil*
> *salt and pepper to taste*
> *fresh sage leaves or dried crushed sage*

Cut the veal or chicken into squares about 1½ inch by 1½ inch. The squares should be ½ to ¾ inches high. Cut the chicken livers in half. Cut the bacon slices in half. Wrap a piece of bacon around each liver. If there is bacon left over, wrap around the mushrooms. On a skewer place a slice of chicken, a sage leaf, the liver and mushrooms. Repeat the layers. This is enough for 2 skewers. Sprinkle with salt and pepper. Dribble with olive oil. Place under the broiler and cook until golden brown and done. Turn once to do the other side. Cooking time will be about 5 minutes on each side. These little "birds" are served with polenta. This will serve 2.

CHICKEN BREASTS WITH PROSCIUTTO AND CHEESE
Petti di pollo con formaggio

This Venetian combination of flavors is outstanding. I like to use it for my "California" Italian dinners. You can assemble it before your guests arrive and have it inthe oven at a low heat while your nibbling your antipasto.

> 4 whole chicken breasts, boned and skin removed
> 8 thin slices of prosciutto
> ¼ lb of fontina, Swiss or jack cheese, sliced thin
> flour
> 1 T. minced fresh sage or 1 T. dry, crushed
> salt and pepper to taste
> Parmesan cheese
> ½ cup white wine
> 3 T. olive oil and 3 T. butter, plus olive oil for the pan

Carefully slice each chicken breast horizontally to make about 4 thin slices (2 from each breast half). Place them between sheets of wax paper and flatten with a meat pounder or the bottom of a heavy bottle. Champagne bottles work well. Sprinkle with salt and pepper and dust with flour.

In a frying pan heat the oil and butter. Lightly brown the pieces on each side. This will take only a few minutes. If you overcook they become dry. In a large baking pan spread a thin layer of olive oil. Place the cooked chicken in the pan. Cut with scissors pieces of the prosciutto to fit the shape of each breast. Sprinkle the sage over the chicken breasts. Place the prosciutto on top of the chicken and top with cheese slices. Swirl the wine around in the pan. Dribble over the chicken. Sprinkle with Parmesan cheese. Lightly cover with foil and place in a 300 degree oven for 15-20 minutes. If you have assembled the dish and it is cold you will need a little longer warming time. This will serve 4.

GRILLED VENETIAN CHICKEN
Pollo alla Griglia

Venetian style grilled chicken always is perfect for any time. Serve garnished with some lemon wedges for that Venice look.

> *one 2-3 lb cut up chicken or parts*
> *¾ cup olive oil*
> *¼ cup lemon juice*
> *1 clove of minced garlic*
> *salt and pepper to taste*
> *1 tsp. crushed red pepper*

Mix all the ingredients except the chicken in a bowl and stir. Place the chicken in the bowl and stir around so all the pieces are coated. Marinate for several hours—or even overnight.

In Venice this chicken is grilled on one of those lovely beds of coals you see in all the restaurant kitchens. In you own home, use a broiler or a barbecue. Place the pieces below the broiler 6-8 inches from the flame. Broil skin side up for 15 minutes and then baste with marinade. Turn and broil 15 minutes on the other side. Baste again. Use this same procedure for the barbecue. Serve garnished with lemon wedges and parsley. This will serve 4-5.

DUCK WITH LEMON PEPPER SAUCE
Anitra con salsa limone pepe

The combination of lemon and pepper is one of the most ancient and favorite of the Venetians. The wealth of Venice was made from pepper. Venice had the monopoly in the trade and distribution of pepper. It was the basic spice of Europe. At one time, over three thousand tons were consumed in a year. Pepper nd lemon combine beautifully with duck.

1-4 to 5 lb duck
1 lemon for the interior of the duck
1 lemon for the juice and rind
3 T. freshly groung black pepper (if pre-ground use a coarse grind)
1 T. olive oil
1 tsp. salt

Rinse the duck off and pat dry with paper towels. Slice one lemon in several slices and place in the cavity of the duck. Sprinkle the inside with a little of the salt and pepper. With cooking string, tie the duck together to hold in the lemon and keep down the end flaps. If you can't find string, unwaxed dental floss may be used.

Squeeze the remaining lemon. Grate the lemon rind into the juice. Add the olive oil, salt and pepper to the lemon mixture.

Rub the duck with this marinade and place on a meat rack in a baking pan. Roast at 325 degrees, basting with the marinade as it cooks. I drain the fat from the pan with a baster, so there won't be too much of a spattery mess. When the duck is tender (in about 2 hours) remove from the pan. Let cool a few minutes and slice in serving pieces. You may add a little flour and stock to the baking pan for gravy, if desired. I cook the neck and giblets separately in a little water with onion, salt and pepper. This can be used for the gravy or soup. This will serve 4.

LIVER VENETIAN STYLE
Fegato alla Veneziana

This is the most famous dish of the Venice cuisine. You will find it on every menu. Usually it is served with polenta. The combination is perfection. This method of cooking, which is a quick stir fry, shows the Oriental influences that are a fascinating part of Venice.

Calf's liver is recommended, but beef liver may also be used. There has always been one burning question that intrigues me: With all the liver used in Venice, where did the rest of the beef go to? Venetians simply do not eat much meat and there is only one liver in each cow. It is a curious situation.

> *1 lb very fresh calf or beef liver*
> *3 white onions, peeled and sliced thin*
> *salt and pepper to taste*
> *3 T. olive oil and 3 T. butter*

Cut the liver in strips about ½ inch wide and 2 inches long. A pair of kitchen scissors will do this easily. Heat the oil and butter in a frying pan and, over a low flame, cook the onions until soft and tender. Remove and set aside. If the oil and butter have dried up, add a little more to fry the liver. Add the liver and stir fry so that it is quickly browned on both sides. Season with salt and pepper. Return the onions and give a final stir. This will serve 3-4.

TONGUE WITH SWEET AND SOUR RAISIN SAUCE
Lingua di bue con agro-dolce

There is a special way of cooking tongue in Venice. They use one of their sweet and sour sauces with raisins. It is really delicious. If you have never tasted tongue cooked this way, you are in for a treat. Grilled polenta is often served with this dish.

1-3 to 3½ lb beef tongue
1½ cups dry red wine
salt and pepper to taste
1 carrot, sliced
1 onion, sliced
1 celery stalk, diced
3 T. flour
3 T. butter
2 T. sugar
2 cups cooking liquid
3 T. red wine vinegar
2 T. golden raisins

Wash the tongue in cool water. Place it in a pot with water to cover. Add the onion, carrot and celery. Season with salt and pepper and add the red wine. Cover and simmer until tender. This will take 2-3 hours. Let the tongue cool in the cooking liquid.

When the tongue is cool enough to handle, remove from the liquid and remove the skin. I like to cook the tongue and keep it refrigerated in the cooking liquid overnight.

Prepare the sauce by melting the butter in a sauce pan. Add the flour (Wondra flour works well) and sugar. Make a little paste. Strain 2 cups of the cooking liquid and add slowly to the paste. Add the raisins, red wine and any additional salt and pepper you might need. Let simmer for 5 minutes. Slice the tongue and pour the sauce over the slices. This will serve 6. Remember, tongue is very nice cold on antipasto platters.

5. FISH & SEAFOOD -
Pesce e Frutta di Mare

SEA BASS COOKED IN WHITE WINE
Branzino al vino bianco

Fish marinated and lightly simmered in white wine is a lovely way to cook any firm fish. Fish cooked this way is also delicious served cold in the summertime.

>*2 lbs sea bass, halibut or any firm fish*
>*¼ cup olive oil*
>*juice of 1 lemon*
>*2 cloves garlic, minced*
>*salt and pepper to taste*
>*1 bay leaf, crumbled*
>*flour*
>*½ cup white wine*
>*2 T. butter and 1 T. olive oil*
>*parsley and lemon wedges for garnish*

In a shallow bowl of glass or china, mix the marinade of olive oil, lemon, garlic, salt and pepper. Cut the fish in 4 serving pieces and place in the marinade. Cover with foil. Marinate for 1-2 hours, turning once during this time.

In a frying pan heat the oil and butter. Remove the fish from marinade. Pat dry with paper towels and dust with flour on both sides. Fry on one side until golden brown and turn to do the other side. Lower the flame and add the marinade and wine. Cover and cook until the fish is done (10-15 minutes). Serve with the pan juices. Garnish with lemon wedges and parsley. This will serve 4.

SHRIMP WITH LEMON AND GARLIC
Scampi con Limone e aglio

This is such a simple and satisfying way to prepare shrimp and one of my favorites. It is easy and quick and you need only a little rice or pasta with salad to complete the dinner. Of course, chilled white wine is a must with this delicate shrimp dinner.

1 lb shrimp, peeled and deveined
3 T. butter
2 T. olive oil
3 cloves garlic, peeled and minced
juice of 1 lemon
salt and pepper to taste
flour

In a frying pan melt the butter and add the oil. Heat to medium hot, Dip the shrimp in the flour just to give a light coating. Place in the pan along with the garlic. Stir fry until the shrimp are cooked. Season with salt and pepper and add the lemon juice. Give a stir around. Serve at once with the lemon sauce on top of the shrimp. This will serve 2-3.

SHRIMP IN A PARMESAN SAUCE
Scampi con salsa Parmigiana

Shrimp tucked in a Parmesan sauce is a special treat. I enjoy this delicate way of preparing shrimp. You can have this dish all prepared ahead, so when your guests arrive all you have to do is put it in the oven. Most other fish dishes require last-minute fussing. I like to use a medium-sized shrimp for this recipe. They are less expensive than the jumbo size and are perfect in the sauce.

1 lb medium-sized shrimp
2 cups half and half
4 T. butter
4 T. flour (I use Wondra)
salt and pepper to taste
½ cup grated Parmesan
¼ cup bread crumbs
butter for baking dish

Clean and peel the shrimp. In a sauce pan melt the butter and blend in the flour to form a paste. Slowly add the half and half. Season with salt and pepper and add the Parmesan. Cook until fairly thick.

Butter a baking dish and place the shrimp in the dish. Pour the sauce over the top. Sprinkle the bread crumbs over the sauce. Bake at 350 degrees for 15-20 minutes, just until the top is light brown. If the dish has been refrigerated add another 10 minutes or so. Don't overcook as everything is really cooked. All you are doing is heating the dish. This will serve 2 generously. Chilled white wine is a must with Shrimp Parmesan.

VENETIAN CRAB SALAD
Granseola Veneto

The large crabs found in the Adriatic have such a fresh, sweet flavorful taste. The Venetians do not like to mask this delicacy by strong flavorings. The crab is just mixed lightly with olive oil and lemon and served in a crab shell. I have found that you can use Alaskan crab and have a similar salad.

> 2 cups cooked crab meat
> 2 T. lemon juice
> 2 T. olive oil
> salt and pepper to taste
> 2 tsp. wine vinegar
> 2 tsp. finely minced green onion tops
> snipped parsley for garnish

Combine the juice, oil, salt, pepper, vinegar and onion in a bowl. Stir to blend. Add the crab and mix gently. Serve in a cleaned crab shell. If you don't have a crab shell, a scallop shell or a lettuce leaf may be used. This will serve 2.

MIXED FRY OF THE SEA
Fritto misto di mare

There is hardly a restaurant in Venice that does not offer a "fritto misto." These are called by various colorful names such as a "Grand Fry of the Adriatic," "Venice Fry,," or a "Lagoon Special." Basically mixed frys are made from the fish that were in the market today and looked attractive to the restaurant fish buyer. Usually squid rings, some little octopus and a small flat fish are included.

When you're making this at home do the same thing; go to your market and buy what looks fresh and bright. There are many batters and ideas of what to dip the fish in before frying. One night in the Zattere section of Venice, in a small local restaurant, I had an especially wonderful fritto misto. After a glass or two of the crisp dry white house wine, I ventured up courage to ask the large, happy cook what his secret batter was. He smiled and simply opened a large wooden drawer filled with flour. This was all he used and I think he had the right secret.

fresh fish, shrimp, squid, scallops, etc.
flour
salt and pepper
lemon wedges
oil for frying (can be a combination of corn oil with olive oil)

You will need ½ lb to ¾ lb fish per person for a generous mixed fry. Dip the pieces in flour seasoned with salt and pepper. Heat the oil to about a ¾-inch height in a frying pan, or if you have a deep fryer you may use this. For occasional use, a frying pan is fine. When the oil is hot, fry the flour-dipped pieces of fish on both sides until golden brown. Do not crowd. You will have to do a couple of batches probably. Place the fried fish on paper towels to drain and keep warm in a 200-degree oven while you complete the frying. Serve garnished with lemon wedges.

GRILLED FISH
Pesce alla griglia

Fish is always very fresh in Venice. There is none of this fresh, frozen, defrosted fish we find in America. The fish is caught and eaten. When you visit the fish market, there is only a smell of the sea. All the treasures of the Adriatic are bright and luminous. Cooking is simple so that all the natural flavors are retained. Venice restaurants usually have wood fire. Grills and chefs are very talented in cooking this way. They know just when to turn the fish. I use my oven broiler or a barbecue grill for this recipe.

> *4 fish steaks (2-2½ lbs) (can be tuna, bass, halibut, salmon, etc.)*
> *¼ cup olive oil*
> *4 T. fresh lemon juice*
> *1 bay leaf, crumbled*
> *salt and pepper to taste*
> *parsley and lemon wedges for garnish*

Mix the oil, lemon, bay leaf, salt and pepper in a shallow dish. Place the fish in the marinade. Put in the refrigerator for 1-2 hours. Turn the steaks once during this period.

Under the broiler or on a grill place the fish. Baste with the marinade while cooking. Cook, turning once, until done. The time will vary with the fish. Fish should not be dry and overcooked. Serve garnished with parsley and lemon. This will serve 4.

VENETIAN SAVORY SOLE
Sogliole in Sapore

This most savory ancient Venetian recipe has an interesting history. It is the traditional dish enjoyed for the Feast of the Redeemer. This is the day when boats go out into the Venetian Lagoon to celebrate the "marriage" of Venice with the sea. The boats are decorated and a ring is thrown into the sea for this symbolic ceremony.

I think this is one of the most fantastic and fascinating of all the fish dishes of the Veneto. A special feature is that it can be eaten hot or cold. You will love the tangy, sweet sour flavor of sole prepared this way.

1 lb sole filets
1 onion, sliced thin
flour
salt and pepper to taste
¼ cup golden raisins
¼ cup pine nuts, lightly toasted
⅓ cup white wine vinegar
olive oil for frying (about ¼ cup)
½ cup white wine to soak the raisins in

Place the raisins in a cup and cover with the wine. Allow to soak for 10 minutes. In a frying pan heat the olive oil. Dip the sole in flour on both sides and sprinkle with salt and pepper. Fry on both sides until golden brown and done. Remove and drain on paper towels in a warm spot. Add the onion to the pan and fry until limp. Then add the raisins and wine they were soaked in and wine vinegar. Stir all together until well blended and slightly reduced. To serve, place the fish on a warm platter and pour the sauce over the top. This will serve 3. You may substitute other fish filets for the sole if desired. If you wish the savory sole cold, just refrigerate. It is lovely for a picnic.

6. PASTA, POLENTA & RICE -
Insalata Pasta, Polenta & Riso

A NOTE ABOUT RISOTTO

On Venetian menus you will find many kinds of risotto. There is no question about it, risotto is a favorite of the Venetians. One must think of risotto as different than the rice dishes of other nations. It is often called "risotto all'ondo" which means with waves. It is true, risotto is rather "wavy." It is not dry but creamy. Sometimes when you are served risotto it can look like a sloppy plop on the plate. This is really the way it should look, so enjoy it. Risotto grows on you.

With the classic risotto you can enjoy many variations. In Venice you will find bits of shrimp or other shellfish. It can have peas or zucchini. If you're using fish or shellfish, often the liquid the fish is cooked in is used for cooking the rice.

Italian short-grained rice can be purchased at any Italian grocery store. I have also used American short-grained rice with risotto recipes. It works quite well. Use your imagination and have some fun creating. To begin you might soak some golden raisins in white wine and stir them into the rice. This is very Venetian and most tasty.

CLASSIC RISOTTA
Risotto classico

With this basic recipe you can serve many variations of tiny tidbits tucked in the rice for tasty surprises. The classic recipe is an elegant dish for any occasion.

1 cup short-grained rice
1 white onion, chopped finely
3-4 cups chicken broth
½ cup dry white wine
2 T. butter
2 T. olive oil
⅓ cup grated Parmesan cheese
salt and pepper to taste

In a heavy saucepan melt the butter and add the olive oil. Over a medium heat add the onions with the rice. Stir around until the rice is coated and the onions a little limp. Add one cup of the broth and stir gently. The rice will begin to absorb the broth. Cook until the broth is nearly absorbed and then add another cup of the broth. I use a wooden spoon and am careful to stir clear to the bottom of the pot so the rice will not stick. Add the remaining cup of broth and again stir. You do not have to stir all the time. When this liquid is absorbed, add the wine and cheese and let cook for a few more minutes. The rice should not be wishy washy tender, but have a slight "give" to each grain. This will serve 4. Risotto should be eaten at once. In Venetian restaurants you may have to wait for this dish. They do not cook it ahead. The cooking time will vary, but usually it takes around 20-25 minutes.

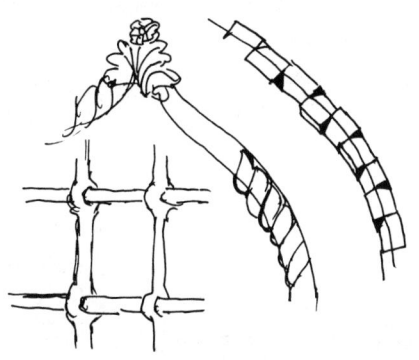

RICE AND PEAS VENICE STYLE
Risi e Bisi alla Veneziana

This classic Venetian dish originated in the 16th century. "Risi and Bisi" were presented to the doge every April 25 to celebrate the feast day of St. Mark. The peas represented the coming of spring and the rice is a symbol of the abundant spring growth.

I have used this rice and peas for light suppers and it is always a favorite with grilled chicken. It is well worth the time to shell fresh peas. Shelling peas is always relaxing and the fresh pea pods have a nice garden scent.

1 white onion, minced
¼ cup butter
1 cup raw Italian or California short-grained rice
2½ cups beef or chicken broth
1 bay leaf
salt and pepper to taste
1 cup fresh peas or 1-10 oz pkg frozen peas
½ cup grated Parmesan cheese

Place half the butter in a heavy sauce pan and melt. Add the minced onion and fry gently until transparent. Add the rice. Stir and fry with the onions for a few minutes. Do not brown; you just want a glassy, limp look. Add the broth, bay leaf, salt and pepper. Stir together. Cover and cook over a low flame for 15 minutes. Remove the cover and stir in the peas. Cover and cook for an additional 10 minutes or until the peas and rice are tender, but not overdone. Stir in the other half of the butter and grated cheese and serve. This will serve 4.

POLENTA RECIPES

Polenta is a cornmeal that has been part of the Veneto cuisine for several hundred years. Cooking polenta in a large copper pot over fireplace coals was a way of life. The polenta was stirred with a wooden stick and cooked for over an hour. The family would talk over the day's events while they waited for the polenta.

I have cooked polenta in many pots and I can say that if you have the time there is something very relaxing about stirring those little golden grains for a long time. You can daydream or chat with someone while you sip some wine. However, sometimes I am short of time and have used a double boiler which works quite well.

Polenta is the perfect accompaniment for many of the Venetian dishes. I have been surprised to find it also goes well with many American foods. Polenta offers a lot of fun to a creative cook. You may buy polenta at Italian stores. American cornmeal may also be used, however it does not have quite the texture of the Italian.

BASIC POLENTA
(stir method)

3 cups of water
1 cup of polenta
1 tsp. salt

In a large pot bring the water to a boil. Reduce flame to a low simmer and slowly with your hand pour in the grains. Some Italians say it should be like little rain drops. Stir with a wooden spoon and when all the grains are in, keep stirring and stirring until the polenta is quite thick. The spoon should stick straight up if put in the center. This will take 30 minutes or more.

DOUBLE BOILER METHOD
In the top of a double boiler place the water and salt. Stir in the polenta and cover. Cook for about 35 minutes until the polenta is solid. Stir once or twice during the cooking.

THE NEXT STEP
After your polenta is done you may serve it immediately with butter and Parmesan cheese—or you may pour it out on a large china platter or on a wooden board. Allow to cool. This may be any amount of time, from 30 minutes to overnight. With cooled polenta you can make any of the following:

Polenta
In Venice the cooled polenta is cut into squares or long bar shapes. It can be fried in a frying pan. Place olive oil in the pan. Put in the polenta and cook each side until golden brown.

You may also broil or grill the polenta. Put a little butter or cheese on top if desired.

A tasty appetizer is polenta with a dab of gorgonzola cheese on the top. This is broiled until the cheese melts.

Thomas Jefferson was quite taken with polenta when he visited Italy. When entertaining at Monticello he often served polenta.

POLENTA WITH MUSHROOM SAUCE
Polenta con salsa funghi

I have become quite a fan of polenta because it can be made into so many exciting flavor combinations. One tasty way of preparing polenta is with this creamy mushroom sauce. You can make this ahead which is handy if you're having guests.

> *1 basic cooked polenta recipe*
> *4 T. butter*
> *4 T. flour*
> *1¾ cups half and half*
> *½ cup white wine*
> *salt and pepper to taste*
> *½ cup grated Parmesan cheese*
> *½ lb fresh mushrooms, sliced*
> *1 green onion, minced*
> *butter for the baking pan*

Cook the polenta from the basic recipe. Pour into an 8×8 baking pan. Refrigerate overnight.

To make the sauce, melt the butter in a saucepan, add the flour and blend. Slowly add the half and half stirring. Add the wine, onion, mushrooms, salt and pepper. Stir until thickish. Blend in the cheese.

Butter an 8×8 baking pan. Cut the polenta into slices about 3½ inches long by ½ inch. Place one layer in the pan and cover with half the sauce. Repeat the layer. Bake at 350 degrees for 25-30 minutes until the top is golden brown and bubbly. This will serve 4 or 5. Cut in squares to serve.

SPAGHETTINI WITH PEAS, EGGS AND PROSCIUTTO
Spaghettini con piselli e uova e prosciutto

Peas are loved by the Venetians. They use them in many ways. I like this recipe for pasta. It is easy to make. Serve with a chilled white wine for a lovely dinner.

> *1 lb pkg spaghettini*
> *3 eggs, beaten*
> *½ cup diced prosciutto or cooked bacon crumbled*
> *1½ cups cooked fresh peas or 1-10 oz pkg frozen petit peas, cooked*
> *¼ cup butter*
> *salt and pepper to taste*
> *½ cup grated Parmesan*

Cook the spaghettini as per package directions. Have ready the eggs, prosciutto, butter and a warm bowl. Drain the pasta and place in the bowl. Immediately beat in with a stirring motion the eggs, prosciutto and butter. The heat will cook the eggs. Season with salt and pepper. Fold in the peas gently. Serve with the grated cheese. This will serve 4-5.

BAKED LASAGNA
Lasagne al forno

All over Italy you will find lasagna. In Venice it is lighter than in southern cities. It has two sauces and may all be prepared ahead. Lasagna makes a nice picnic dish. You heat it, wrap it in a clean large bath towel and wrap some newspapers around the towel. It will keep warm for an hour. Serve with some salad, wine and fresh fruit for a terrific picnic.

> 1 T. olive oil
> 1 onion, chopped
> 1 clove garlic, minced
> ½ lb ground veal or Italian sausage
> 1-15 oz can tomato sauce
> ½ cup white wine
> salt and pepper to taste

In a saucepan heat the oil. Lightly brown the onion, garlic and meat. Add the white wine and tomato sauce. Season with salt and pepper. Cook over a low flame for 20 minutes. This is your first sauce. This can be used for any pasta and freezes well.

This is your second sauce;

> 2 cups half and half
> 3 T. flour
> 3 T. butter
> salt and pepper to taste
> ¼ tsp. nutmeg

Melt the butter and make a paste with the flour. Slowly add the half and half and seasonings. Stir over a low flame until smooth.

> 8 oz green or white lasagna noodles
> ½ lb grated Parmesan
> ¼ lb sliced Mozzarella

Cook the noodles as per package directions and drain. Rub a baking dish with some olive oil. Lay a layer of the noodles. Next a layer of the red sauce add then the white with the mozzarella and then the parmesan. Repeat layers. Bake at 350 degrees for 25 minutes. This will serve 6.

7. VEGETABLES -
Legumi

GRANDMOTHER'S STYLE ZUCCHINI
Zucchini alla Nonna

This is one of those "homey" dishes like grandmothers make. It is simple, easy and a terrific addition to any meal.

> *1 lb fresh zucchini*
> *1 onion, sliced*
> *salt and pepper to taste*
> *2 eggs, beaten lightly*
> *¼ cup Parmesan cheese*
> *3 T. olive oil and 3 T. butter*

Cut the zucchini in strips about 2 inches long and ½ inch wide. In a frying pan heat the oil. Place the zucchini and onion in the pan and stir fry until tender. This is best not overcooked. Season with salt and pepper. Add the eggs with the cheese and give a few more stirs so the eggs will cook. Serve at once. This will serve 2 for a light main dish or 4 for a side vegetable dish.

SPINACH WITH GOLDEN RAISINS
Spinaci con Uvetta

Pretty fresh green spinach cooked quickly with plumped golden raisins is an exciting combination. Venetians seem to have a passion for "Uvetta" and enjoy adding them to many dishes in their cuisine. Frozen spinach may be used, but fresh is preferred.

1 bunch fresh spinach or 1-10 oz pkg frozen leaf
¼ cup golden raisins
½ cup dry white wine
2 T. olive oil
salt and pepper to taste
tiny pinch of nutmeg

Wash the spinach. An Italian lady told me about saving the spinach stems. I always had put them in the compost. These stems are tasty and may be cooked in a little olive oil and liquid. So if you wish save the stems for later use after you cut them from the spinach leaf.

Cook the spinach leaves. This is done in Italy with only the water that is left clinging to the leaves after washing. You will be surprised there is enough liquid on the spinach to cook without burning. Cook covered with salt and pepper just until tender and still green.

Soak the raisins in the wine for 30 minutes or so. Drain the cooked spinach and rinse the pan it was cooked in. Add to the pan over a low heat the olive oil. Add the cooked spinach with a pinch of nutmeg. Drain the raisins (the wine may be used for soup or another marinade). Add the raisins and give a stir. Serve hot. This will serve 3.

FRIED ZUCCHINI
Zucchine fritte

If someone gives you a little plate of fried zucchini, it is so good that in a few minutes you will find it is all gone. I love to nibble on fried zucchini at any hour. Sometimes there is a thick coating on it that I don't like. The batter that is perfect for fried zucchini is called "pastella." It is a simple little flour and water mixture. You may use it to fry any other vegetables.

> 1 lb medium-sized zucchini
> 1 cup water
> $2/3$ cup flour
> salt and pepper to taste
> olive oil or corn oil for frying

Wash the zucchini and cut into lengthwise sticks. They will look like french fries or if you wish, they can be a little larger.

In a bowl pour the water and blend in the flour stirring until you have a smooth mixture. Add the desired salt and pepper. Dry the slices of zucchini. In a frying pan heat the oil. You don't need a lot, usually ½ inch to ¾ inch is enough for this shallow frying. Dip the zucchini in the batter and fry until golden brown on both sides in the oil. Sometimes the dish is sprinkled with Parmesan cheese. Drain on paper towels and serve right away. This will serve 4.

SAUCED ASPARAGUS
Asparagi con salsa

This is a Venice springtime treat. The asparagus is cooked lightly and then covered with a Bechamel sauce topped by a few toasted walnuts. It looks lovely and is an ideal taste combination.

1 lb fresh asparagus
2 T. butter
2 T. flour
1 cup milk or half and half
½ cup grated Parmesan cheese
½ tsp. Dijon mustard
salt and pepper to taste
2 T. lightly toasted walnuts, chopped

Wash the asparagus and snap off the lower part of the stem where they break easily. You can save these for soup. I have a friend who trims and peels the stems so they look neat. She then chills them and nibbles the stems like you would a carrot or celery stick.

Cook the asparagus covered with lightly salted water until barely tender. Overcooking destroys both texture and flavor.

Make the sauce by melting the butter in a saucepan. Add the flour to make a paste. Gradually add the milk. Slowly stir in the cheese, salt, pepper and mustard. Stir until the mixture is slightly thick. Drain the asparagus. Pour the sauce over asparagus. Garnishing with the walnuts. This will serve 4.

SWEET AND SOUR ONIONS
Cipolline agrodolce

This sweet and sour taste has been used in Venetian recipes for centuries. These little onions are good either hot or cold. This recipe is only for two, but can certainly be doubled or tripled. You might want to use it for a Thanksgiving dinner addition.

> *1 cup little boiling or pearl onions*
> *1 slice bacon, diced*
> *3 T. olive oil*
> *½ cup red wine vinegar*
> *¼ cup white wine*
> *2 T. sugar*
> *salt and pepper to taste*

Peel the onions. In a frying pan heat the oil. Place the onions and bacon in the pan and stir fry for a few minutes. You want the onions glazed. Add the remaining ingredients. Cover and cook over a low flame 10-15 minutes just until the onions are tender. Serve with the sweet and sour sauce.

MASHED POTATOES WITH PARMESAN CHEESE
Patate puree alla Parmigiano

You may not think of the Venetians using many potatoes in their cooking. They do, however, enjoy this special treatment of potatoes, mashed with butter, milk and cheese and topped with additional cheese. This is another dish that can be made ahead and will only need a little warming in the oven.

2 lbs potatoes
¼ cup melted butter
¾ to 1 cup milk or half and half
2 egg yolks
salt and pepper to taste
¼ tsp. nutmeg
¾ cup grated Parmesan cheese (reserve ¼ for topping)
olive oil for pan

Peel the potatoes and cook in boiling salted water until tender. Drain the potatoes and with a mixer or by hand, mix in the remaining ingredients. The amount of liquid will depend on the potatoes. The mixture should be creamy. Rub a baking pan with olive oil and place the potatoes in the pan. Top with the remaining cheese. Bake in a 350 degree oven for 15-20 minutes until the top is golden brown and the potatoes nice and hot. If you have refrigerated this dish, allow extra baking time. This will serve 6.

MUSHROOMS WITH GARLIC
Funghi con aglio

This is a quick and uncomplicated way to prepare mushrooms. These may be served hot, room temperature or cold as part of an antipasto platter. The quick cooking preserves the essence of mushroom flavor.

1 lb mushrooms
2 cloves garlic, peeled and minced
2 T. olive oil
salt and pepper to taste
¼ cup white wine
½ tsp. dried red pepper (optional)

In a frying pan warm the olive oil. Slice the mushrooms and add to the pan with the garlic. Add salt and pepper and the red pepper if used. Stir fry for just a few minutes until the mushrooms are tender but not overdone. Add the white wine to the pan and give another stir around. You will find this recipe has many uses. Extra mushrooms may be used in salad, a sandwich or pizza.

8. PIZZA & SANDWICHES

PIZZA IN VENICE
Pizza alla Veneto

Zattere is the section of Venice that faces the island of Giudecca. If you want pizza in Venice, come to one of the many outdoor cafes in this area. It is one of the delights of Venice to sit and watch the water life and nibble a hot fresh pizza with a carafe of local wine.

There are all the traditional flavors of pizza served in Venice. Some of the delicious seafood combinations are typically Venetian and always worth ordering. Venetians also like a topping with gorgonzola cheese.

Basic pizza dough
1 pkg dry yeast (¼ oz)
1 cup warm water
1 tsp. sugar
1 tsp. salt
2 T. olive oil
2 cups flour plus about 1½ cups more

Dissolve the yeast in water. Remember the water should be just warm—not hot. Stir until the yeast is dissolved. Add the sugar, salt and olive oil. Stir in 2 cups of sifted flour and after that is blended in, add the additional 1½ cups more of sifted flour. Knead for a few minutes to get all the ingredients well blended. Form in a ball and place in a lightly greased bowl. Cover with a dampened towel and set in a warm place to rise.

When the dough has doubled (this will take about 45 minutes) punch the dough down. Remove from the bowl and roll out in desired size pizza shapes. This will make 5 or 6-9 inch pizzas. Bake at 400 degrees 10-15 minutes with any of the following toppings:

VENETIAN PIZZA TOPPINGS

The Italian word "misto" is greatly used in Venetian food. It simply means mixed. There is no doubt Venetian chefs have great fun arranging and mixing various items on the top of pizzas. They usually begin with a thin spreading of tomato sauce or sliced fresh, peeled or crushed canned tomatoes. First on top of the unbaked crust a quick brushing of olive oil is done. Next the tomato. Now you are ready for the mixed creations.

These are some of the ingredients used in Venice. They may be used as one item or as the Venetians do, mix several kinds of toppings.

> *Italian sausage, crumbled*
> *sardines, canned or fresh*
> *mozzarella cheese—grate for even distribution*
> *eggplant, partly cooked, cubed or thin slices*
> *olives*
> *capers*
> *Gorgonzola cheese*
> *mushrooms, sliced*
> *prosciutto*
> *anchovies*
> *red or white onions slices*
> *garlic, peeled and minced*
> *shrimp, cooked*
> *clams, minced*
> *mussels, cooked and sliced or cut in small pieces*
> *seasonings are black pepper, salt, oregano and basil*

Pizza does not have to be complicated. Once in one of my children's cooking classes, after we had made pizza from "scratch", a young girl said, "Why do all that? My mother just puts Ragu on an English muffin."

SANDWICHES

One of my favorite walks in Venice is in the streets around the Accademia. This is one of the student areas of the city. Students in any land are always hungry. I would watch them go into the cafes for coffee and sandwiches. One cafe had all of one side devoted to sandwiches. Two sandwich makers did nothing else but make these marvelous fresh creations all day long. I first went in just to look at the scene. It was only a few seconds before I succumbed and ordered a sandwich. It was sliced marinated mushrooms with a soft mozzarella. The bread used is a firm white. The bread has a good homey taste. It is spread with mayonnaise before the ingredients are added. It will be served to you sliced in half in two triangles with a napkin.

This sandwich was so good and a perfect tasty mid-morning or afternoon snack; I began enjoying sandwiches all over Venice. I found they are very popular and certainly more healthy for you than most American snacks. Soon I decided, why not abandon the hotel breakfast which is usually a long wait for a roll and coffee. Instead of hanging around the hotel, plunge yourself into the streets and look for the first bar-cafe. Here will be the locals and in a glass case, fresh sandwiches. It is not only better than the hotel situation, but cheaper and more fun.

My sandwich research led me to notice that around 11:00 in the morning housewives would gather for a bit of morning gossip over a glass of wine and a sandwich. The glass of wine is small and called an Ombra. It is served usually in a pretty Venetian glass. I like this Venice custom.

VENETIAN SANDWICH FILLINGS

The various fillings are placed in stainless steel square containers so they are all ready for the assembly line.

Some of the foods used are:

Eggplant and Prosciutto - the sliced eggplant has been cooked.
Tomato and Mozzarella - the fresh tomato is sliced the same size as the cheese; sometimes a fresh basil leaf is added.
Tuna and egg - the tuna is mashed with mayonnaise and the egg is hard boiled and sliced.
Russian salad - a light layer of salad with a lettuce leaf.
Hard-boiled egg and lettuce - the egg is sliced with fresh black pepper ground on top with lettuce.
Pepperoni - slices are placed on the mayonnaise; salami is also used.
Artichoke hearts and cheese - the hearts are sliced thin with a provolone cheese slice.
Sardine - they are mashed with a little mayonnaise.
Shrimp and Parmesan - little marinated bay shrimp with grated Parmesan.

Any of these fillings may be mixed with others. You could even have a sandwich lunch party with this Venetian idea.

9. DESSERTS -
Dolci

CHOCOLATE AND WALNUT CAKE
Torta di noci e cioccolato

Italian cakes are flatter than American cakes. They are flavorful and smaller slices are served. This cake is quite simple to make. You do need a spring form pan. These pans are available at any kitchen store and handy for many things.

½ cup butter, room temperature
1 cup sugar
3 oz semi-sweet chocolate (3 squares)
¾ cup strong coffee
2 eggs
2 T. rum
2 cups flour
1 tsp. baking powder
¼ tsp. salt
2 cups chopped walnuts

Cream the butter with the sugar. Melt the chocolate in the coffee. Cool slightly. Add to the butter sugar mixture. Beat in the eggs and rum. Sift the flour, baking powder and salt together. Add to the batter along with the chopped walnuts. Place in a 10-inch spring form pan. Bake at 350 degrees for 35-40 minutes until firm. Remove from pan and cool on a rack. Sometimes whipped cream is spread on the top. This will serve 8.

PEARS POACHED IN RED WINE
Pere al vino rosso

Pears that are poached in red wine are glistening and lovely. This is one of the most refreshing of all Italian desserts. In Venice a Barolo or Merlot wine is often used. You may use any good dry red wine. An added attraction for this recipe is that when you're poaching the pears, your kitchen will be filled with a lovely scent.

> *4 ripe pears (bartletts work well)*
> *1 lemon, juice and grated rind*
> *3 cups dry red wine*
> *1 cup sugar*
> *1 tsp. cinnamon*

Peel the pears. Leave the stem on. Place in a saucepan the lemon juice, rind, wine, sugar and cinnamon. Add the pears. Bring the mixture to a simmer and give a stir. Cover and cook for about 10 minutes. The pears should just be barely tender. Watch carefully that you don't overcook. If the liquid does not completely cover the pears while cooking, just roll them around so all sides will be coated. Cool in the syrup. These may be served at room temperature or chilled. This will serve 4.

VENICE STYLE SICILIAN CAKE
Cassata alla Veneto

There is a Sicilian connection in Venice. There has always been a commercial trade and an exchange of foods. Both places are surrounded by seas and have been exposed to spices and sweets from around the world. Cassata is a traditionally Sicilian dessert the Venetians like to enjoy. In this version the Venetians have added golden raisins. Golden raisins are a favorite of this city.

1 pound cake, 9×5×3 homemade or from a bakery
1-15 oz carton of Ricotta cheese (about 2 cups)
¼ cup cream
¼ cup chopped semi-sweet chocolate
¼ cup orange flavored liqueur (Curaco, Cointreau, etc.)
¾ cup golden raisins
¼ cup rum
frosting:
12 oz semi-sweet chocolate
¾ cup strong coffee
1 cup sweet butter

Cut the pound cake horizontally into ½ inch slices. Place one layer of cake on a cake platter. You want a square cake when finished, so you may have to slice off the top if it is rounded. Combine the ricotta with the cream and chocolate. Soak the raisins in the rum for 15 minutes to "plump" them. Add to the ricotta with the liqueur and mix well. Spread this on top of the cake slices and repeat the cake layer with the ricotta topping. Do not put the ricotta on top of the final cake layer. The cake may be a little wiggly but just straighten it up. Cover with plastic wrap and place in the refrigerator.

Make the frosting by melting the chocolate in the coffee. You might want to cut the chocolate in smaller pieces for easier melting. When the chocolate is melted break the butter in small pieces and add, piece by piece, to the chocolate mixture. Stir after each addition. When all the butter is added, chill the frosting until it is thick enough to spread (about 30 minutes). Frost sides and top of cake with this luscious frosting. Cover the cake and let it mellow for 1 or 2 days before serving it. This will serve 8. My daughter Suzanne always wants it for her birthday.

PEARS FILLED WITH CHEESE
Pere Ripiene

Fruit for dessert is always on Venetian tables. During the pear season this combination of cheese and pears is very popular.

> 4 ripe pears
> juice of 1 lemon
> ¼ cup of Gorgonzola (or bleu) cheese at room temperature
> 2 T. butter at room temperature
> 2 T. finely chopped walnuts

Peel the pear and cut in half lengthwise. Leave the stem attached to one of the pear halves if you want a whole pear per person. Remove the pear core and seeds. Scoop out about a tablespoon of the pear center of each pear half. This is to make a little pocket for the cheese filling.

Rub the pears with the lemon juice. This will keep them from turning brown. Mash the cheese and butter together. Fill each pear hollow with about 1 tsp. of the filling. If you want a whole pear per person, gently fit the two halves together and roll in the nuts. For a half per person, leave the halves separate and roll in the nuts. Chill slightly and serve. This will serve 4 to 8.

MACEDONIA OF MIXED FRUIT
Macedonia di frutta misto

You might wonder why a beautiful bowl of various fruits in a Venice restaurant is called Macedonia. Macedonia was an area of many mixed groups of people in Greece. A chef explained to me that Alexander the Great was able to take all these diverse people and combine them happily into one kingdom. This is the principle behind this dish. You take fresh fruits and combine them. It is traditionally a mixture where one flavor does not overpower the others. The amount of fruits needs to be of fairly equal amounts. Most recipes call for the addition of Maraschino liqueur, but you may use cointreau, Grand Marnier or some other fruit liqueur if you can't find Maraschino.

3 lbs (approximately) of assorted fruits such as:

2 bananas
2 apples
2 peaches
2 pears
melons, apricots, plums, berries, etc.
1½ cups freshly squeezed orange juice
grated rind of one lemon
½ cup sugar
¼ cup fruit liqueur

The idea is to use whatever fruit is in season. If you are using berries, do not add them until the last minute as they will tend to become mushy. Raspberries are lovely in this mixture.

In a bowl mix the orange juice, lemon rind, sugar and liqueur. Cut the fruits you use in bite-sized slices or squares. Add to the juices and stir around gently. This may be done several hours ahead. The amount of people this will serve varies, depending on if you are serving it for a lunch fruit salad or dessert. For dessert it should serve 6-8.

YELLOW DIAMOND CORNMEAL COOKIES
Zaletti-Gialletti

This is a happy, bright cookie. In the local dialect of Venice "zaletti" is a name for these yellow (gialetti) little cookies. These cookies are a specialty of Venice. They are very nice to serve with a white wine like an Italian chilled Soave.

¾ cup golden raisins
¼ cup rum
2 eggs
¾ cup sugar
grated rind of 1 lemon
¾ cup melted butter
1 cup fine cornmeal
¼ tsp. salt
1 tsp. vanilla
½ cup pine nuts
butter for baking sheet
confectioner's sugar

Place the raisins in the rum to soften them. This takes about 15 minutes. Melt the butter and set aside. With an electric mixer or by hand with a wooden spoon, beat the eggs with the sugar until well blended. Add the vanilla and lemon rind. Sift the cornmeal with the flour and salt. Add alternately with the melted butter blending well. Drain the raisins and add with the pine nuts to the batter. Heat the oven to 350 degrees.

Place the batter on a floured board and pat with your hands or a rolling pin the dough to make a square about ¼ inch thick. With a diamond cutter or your hands make diamond-shaped cookies and place on a buttered cookie sheet. Bake at 350 degrees for 10 minutes or until the cookies are golden brown. Of course you may make any shape you want, but diamonds are the traditional form. This will make 3 dozen Zaletti.

ITALIAN LEMON PIE
Crostata al limone

This airy, tangy light pie is such a refreshing dessert. Italian pie crust is different than the American crust. It has white wine added for a zesty flavor. The dough is called pasta frolla.

Pasta frolla:
1½ cups all purpose flour
pinch of salt
½ cup sweet butter, room temperature
1 egg
3 T. sugar
3-4 T. chilled white wine

Lemon filling:
4 eggs (room temperature), separated
½ cup sugar
⅓ cup fresh lemon juice
grated rind of 1 lemon

Prepare the crust by placing the flour and salt in a bowl. Add the butter and with a pastry blender, cut it until the mixture resembles a coarse meal. Beat the egg with a fork and add, with the wine, to the dough. Blend together. Place on a board and gather up with your hands. Knead a couple times and make a ball. Place the ball of dough in the refrigerator to rest for at least an hour. It can rest up to 4 hours. Roll out on a floured board to make a circle to fit a 9 or 10-inch pie pan. Place in the pan.

To make the filling, beat the egg yolks with the sugar until thickish. Remove to a double boiler. Add the lemon juice and rind. Cook over a low heat stirring until thick. Set aside to cool. Beat the whites until soft peaks form. Very carefully blend into the cooled yolk mixture. Place in the pie pan. Smooth the top. Bake at 350 deg. for 30-35 minutes until the top is light brown. This will serve 6. It can be served chilled or at room temperature. There is usually a little pie dough left over. It can be used for a little tart or something.

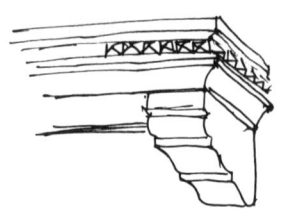

BAKED STUFFED PEACHES
Pesche ripine al forno

This pretty dessert is one of those flavorful and attractive sweets that can be easily popped in the oven while you're cooking dinner. It is best served slightly warmed. You may have it all prepared ahead ready for cooking. If you haven't tasted summer ripe peaches prepared in this Italian way, you have been missing one of summer's delights.

6 large ripe peaches
½ cup macaroon cookie crumbs
1 egg
grated rind of one lemon
½ cup sugar
2 T. butter
½ cup white wine

Carefully cut the peaches in half and remove the seeds. When you remove the seeds make a little scoop indentation in each peach half. You want to remove just a little peach flesh so that you have a nice little "nest" in which to put the stuffing.

Mash the small amount of peach flesh you have removed with the cookie crumbs. Lightly beat the egg and add to this peach and cookie mixture with the lemon rind and sugar. Place the peaches in a baking dish and fill each "nest" with the stuffing. Dot with the butter. Bake uncovered at 350 degrees for 20-25 minutes until the stuffing is slightly brown and peaches tender. This will serve 6.

10. VISITING VENICE

VISITING VENICE

Part of the fun of any voyage is the planning and anticipation for the adventure. There are some things to think about for your Venice visit. The time of the year is important. Try to avoid summer as Venice is very crowded. In spite of the crowds summer is time for bathing at the Lido and outdoor music in the piazza San Marco. Spring and fall are the best times for a visit. Winter has a special light and moods.

It is essential to make hotel reservations far ahead. Venice is one of the most popular places to visit in the world. I have been with friends, carrying luggage, walking down the streets looking for a hotel room. This is not much fun on vacation. Making reservations is easy. Simply pick a couple of hotels, write airmail to them (this can be done in English). Ask the price and mention if you want a double room with a bath, etc. The hotels will write you back and usually ask for a small deposit to keep the room for you.

I like to have a map before arriving in a city. There are many good guide books written about Venice with maps and all the information you need to find your way around. Buy one before you leave.

If you get lost in Venice all you need to do is look up on the building walls. There will be a painted arrow directing you to San Marco, Rialto and other landmarks.

When you travel to Venice by train look out the windows before you get to the city. You will see the farm fields turn into marsh and then the marsh turn into the lagoon waters. It is exciting. After you leave the train you walk out on a large platform where the "water buses" vaporetti stop. They are always crowded so one must stand in line and be patient. The view is wonderful. Usually your hotel will tell you what number to take. The private water taxis are quite expensive so save your money for the gondola ride after you are settled.

There is one thing while you are in Venice that you should not miss and that is a gondola ride. Skimming and floating along the Venetian canals in a gondola is something you will never forget. Sunset I think is the best time because you can see the deep green shadows in the canals and the changing sky. Night is lovely too. There are lanterns on the gondolas and the sounds of gondoliers singing Italian folk songs for the tourist groups. Please do not worry about the price. Prices are regulated and the gondoliers are quite gallant, honest, fascinating men. Rides are a little more in the night than in the daytime. Gondola rides are one of the things in life that you should not ruin by worrying about the lira. It is possible and recommended to take along some chilled wine or champagne with you to sip along the canals.

Guide books will give the latest information on museum hours and practical information. There is, however, one thing that not all of them stress and that is a visit to Torcello.

Torcello is called the "mother of Venice" because that is where the first tribes fleeing the mainland settled. It was from Torcello that they slowly moved to Venice. To reach Torcello you can take the vaporetto from the Fondamenta Nuove. The weekends are a good time to go because you will see the locals heading for "a day in the country." Torcello is rather like the country. When you arrive it is marshy with a brick path leading you to the center of the city. There is an excellent Museo del "Estuario" and the ancient cathedral. You will see people plopping down tablecloths and eating on grassy spots. There are several restaurants. Harry Cipriani has his "Locando Cipriani" here. You can dine among the garden flowers. The food is outstanding and "country" dining at its best.

If you have the time, a boat ride down the Brenta Canal is very memorable. The trip is taken in a special boat called "Il Burchiello." It is modeled after the 17th century boats that would bring the Venetians to the villas that line the banks of the canal. Music was played on the boats and parties and dancing were waiting at the villas. Stops are made to visit several of the villas and time for a delicious lunch at a waterside restaurant. This ride can be taken from Venice to Padua or Padua to Venice. If you do want to spend the night in Padua, a bus will take you back to Venice. If you need the exact time and location check with your travel agent or the Italian tourist office.

There are always exciting theatre, music and art events happening in Venice. Many of them are not always listed in the usual tourist newspapers. Keep your eyes on the walls. Suddenly a new poster will be pasted to the wall announcing a wonderful performance. It was from a poster that I found out there was a night concert in St. Marks. The church was lighted so one could view those ancient and marvelous mosaics while listening to chorale music.

La Fenice is the gem of the world's opera houses. There is usually some musical happening going on even if it is not the opera season. Tickets can be purchased right at the opera house during the day.

Souvenir shopping is not my favorite thing. I would rather sit in a little piazza with a glass of wine or coffee and watch the people. There is one thing, however, that is easy to buy and pack in Venice. That is beads. They are so beautiful and not costly. I also love the little tourist carnival masks. There are many curious faces and expressions. I could not resist a small leather mask that has a big hook nose with a wart and sardonic smile. Fans are another Venetian favorite tourist item. You may be tempted to buy a Murano glass chandelier, but I have always worried it might be difficult to pack.

Everyone enjoys buying grain and feeding the pigeons. This makes a classic photograph for your album when the visit to Venice has ended.

SUGGESTED HOTELS AND RESTAURANTS IN VENICE

I am always hesitant about recommendations. Sometimes people do not have the same wonderful experiences as I did. The cook may be in a bad mood. The hotel clerk might be tired from the night before. Humans after all run hotels and restaurants and everyone has their ups and downs.

HOTELS
Gritti Palace, 2467 San Marco, Santa Maria del Giglio.
One of the grand hotels with dining on the terrace.
Danielli, 4196 Castello, Riva degli Schiavoni.
This was a 15th century palazzo and is one of the great luxury hotels of Venice.
Concordia, 367 San Marco, Calle Larga, San Marco.
When I stayed here I could see and hear the bells of San Marco. A well run hotel.
Saturnia e International, 2398 San Marco, Calle Larga XXII Marzo.
A good location with 2 fine restaurants: Il Cortile and La Caravella.
La Fenice et des Artistes, 1936 San Marco, Campiello de la Fenice.
If you love music and want to be near La Fenice opera house, this is the place to be.
La Calcina, 780 Dorsoduro, Fondamenta Zattere dei Gesuati.
This is a small pensione where John Ruskin stayed while he worked on the "Stones of Venice." It is a wonderful location and most friendly staff.
Londra Palace, 4171 Castello, Riva degli Schiavoni.
Great views of the lagoon. The Do Leoni Hotel Restaurant has an excellent menu and food.

RESTAURANTS

Al Graspo de Ua, 5093 San Marco, Calle dei Bombaseri.
The fish is terrific and you will find all the Venetian specialties.
Montin, 1147 Dorsoduro, Fondamento diBorgo.
You can dine in their lovely garden. Paintings are on the walls inside. I had a wonderful duck with polenta.
Alla Madonna, 594 San Polo, Calle della Madonna.
Go on weekends and see all the Italian families enjoying the fresh fish and having fun.
San Trovaso, 1016 Dorsoduro, Fondamenta Priuli.
Good neighborhood food and excellent pizza.
Harry's Bar, 1323 San Marco, Calle Vallaresso.
This is a must. Of course there are tourists along with the Venetians. Anything you choose is perfectly cooked with the finest ingredients.
Harry's Dolci, 773 Giudecca (on the Giudecca island).
You can sit outdoors and watch the canal with the boats and birds. I had one of the best cannelloni in the world and a terrific figi crostini.
La Colomba, 1665 San Marco-Frezzeria.
Take time to look at all the fine art in the restaurant. This is always very crowded and popular with very good food.
Al Teatro, 1916 San Marco, Campo San Fantin.
This is one of my favorites because the menu offers so many good things. It is open until midnight so you can have a pizza or one of their excellent soups after the opera. When the weather is warm and the talbes are filled, they will just add another table for you. The staff is very friendly.
Trattoria Al Columbo, S. Luca 4620.
This restaurant is frequented by Venetians. The location is handy, near the theatres, and the food traditional and cooked perfectly.

INDEX

A note about risotto, 53
Baked lasagna, 60
Baked stuffed peaches, 86
Barley and bean soup, 17
Basic polenta, 59
Bean and pasta soup, 15
Beef raw filet with mustard sauce, 10
Beef roast cooked in red wine, 30
Celery rice and sausage soup, 16
Chicken breasts with prosciutto and cheese, 36
Chicken broth with cheese cubes, 18
Chicken livers on toast, 4
Chocolate and walnut cake, 79
Classic risotto, 54
Duck with lemon pepper sauce, 38
Escaped birds, 35
Flat Italian meatballs with lemon, 31
Fried zucchini, 63
Fried cheese, 9
Grandmother's style zucchini, 63
Grilled fish, 48
Grilled Venetian chickeh, 37
Hard-boiled eggs stuffed with spinach, 6
Italian lemon pie, 85
Lettuce salad with farmer's dressing, 26
Little beef steaks with red onions, 29
Little shrimp toast, 8
Liver Venetian style, 39
Macedonia of mixed fruits, 83
Mashed potatoes with Parmesan cheese, 68
Mixed fry of the sea, 47
Mushrooms with garlic, 69
Pavese style soup, 14
Pears filled with cheese, 80
Pizza in Venice, 73
Polenta with mushroom sauce, 58
Polenta recipes, 56
Pork chops with wine and lemon, 34
Pork cooked in milk, 35
Prosciutto with bread sticks, 3

Prosciutto with melon, 7
Rice and peas Venice style, 55
Romaine salad with red onions, 21
Russian salad, 22
Sardine fingers, 5
Sandwiches, 75
Sauced asparagus, 66
sandwiches, 75
Sea bass cooked in white wine, 43
Shrimp with lemon and garlic, 44
Shrimps in a Parmesan sauce, 45
Spagettini with peas, eggs and prosciutto, 59
Spinach with golden raisins, 66
Suggested hotels and restaurants, 92–93
Sweet and sour onions, 67
Tomato and basil Summer salad, 23
Tongue with sweet and sour raisin sauce, 40
Veal in lemon and wine sauce, 32
Venetian bean soup, 13
Venetian crab salad, 46
Venetian Pizza toppings, 74
Venetian sandwich fillings, 76
Venetian savory sole, 49
Veneto string bean salad, 24
Venetian style Sicilian cake, 81
Visiting Venice, 89–91
Yellow diamond cornmeal cookies, 84

Biography

Betty Evans was born in Pasadena, California. Her interest in Italian food began in the sixties when she lived in Italy for two years with her family. She studied Italian at the Universita Per Stranieri in Perugia. While living in Italy she collected recipes and did special research on Italian regional cooking.

Venice has been her favorite cuisine. She has visited this city several times since the sixties. In the fall of 1985 she stayed in Venice to complete ideas for this book. Her husband Gordon did the sketches during this time.

Betty lives in Hermosa Beach, where she is food editor for the *Easy Reader* and teaches cooking classes. Her first book, *California Cooking with Betty Evans,* was published in 1985. South Bay News Reel, a popular television program on channel 10 in the Los Angeles area, is featuring Betty Evans in a weekly cooking segment.

In addition to her food interests, she is an honorary docent at the Natural History Museum of Los Angeles and was Woman of the Year in Hermosa Beach.

Mail Order Information:

For additional copies of COOKING WITH BETTY EVANS books send $6.95 per book plus $1.50 for shipping and handling. In California add 6½% sales tax. Make checks payable to Betty Evans, 1769 Valley Park Avenue, Hermosa Beach, California 90254 Telephone (213) 379-5932.

VENICE, ITALY, COOKING WITH BETTY EVANS $6.95
CALIFORNIA COOKING WITH BETTY EVANS $6.95

Also avilable through local bookstores that use R.R. Bowker Company BOOKS IN PRINT catalogue system. Order through publisher SUNFLOWER INK for bookstore discount.